C000093297

BIGFOOT
AND
DOGMAN
SIGHTINGS
2

Assembled and rewritten by

Richard Hunt

BIGFOOT AND DOGMAN SIGHTINGS
2

Copyright © 2022 Richard Hunt

All rights reserved.

Do not copy any content within this
book without first getting the author's
permission.

Be Aware

The stories within this book are eyewitness reports; hence Richard cannot substantiate the claims; however, he took every measure to ensure that these testimonies presented original and consistent details. Richard believes wholeheartedly in the following stories. Given that he, himself, has seen sasquatch, he's confident in his ability to detect the legitimacy of other reports.

Privacy Agreement

It's no surprise that so many people who submitted stories wish to keep their identities private. It's never been so easy to have your public image ruined by a mob of weak-minded individuals who do nothing but attack others on the internet. For that reason, I discouraged the ones who volunteered to share personal information, explaining that even if they didn't mind, they might have friends and family that could potentially face future ridicule.

Do You Have a Story to Tell?

I'm always looking for new bigfoot and dogman sighting reports. If you've seen these creatures in the flesh, please don't hesitate to send me an email with as many details as you can recall. I thank you in advance. You can write me at the following email address:

RichardHuntBigfoot@gmail.com

Contents

-My Dogs Ran for the Hills-

Location: Tillamook, Oregon

Submitted by: Craig W.

Not long after I divorced my wife, I moved from Northern California to a small town in Oregon called Tillamook. I had grown desperate to relocate to where I wouldn't see anyone I knew. My ex-wife and I were

1

socialites, and it seemed like a day couldn't go by where I didn't cross paths with a familiar face. Something about the separation made me lose all ambition to spend time with other people, at least around the beginning.

Since I wasn't sure how long I'd want to hide out or how long it would take for my emotions to recover, I decided to rent instead of purchase. It had for quite some time been a romanticized idea of mine to live in the woods. I wanted to wake up to wind chimes, birds chirping, and all that other good stuff. I also liked the idea of living in a place where there wasn't the best cellular reception. I wanted to minimize how often I browsed social media, checked emails, etc. In other words, I intended that stage of my life to be about me and me alone.

Well, I started feeling a bit lonely soon after settling into my new place. Because of that, I concluded that the best treatment would be not to get just one but two dogs. Yes, my state of mind seemed to have made me more impulsive than usual. I scooped up the dogs from a local shelter. Since they were mutts, I'm not sure what breeds they were, but it was easy to tell that they both had some Pitbull DNA.

After moving to the area, it immediately became my hobby to take my dogs for long walks throughout nearby trails. There were many within a ten-mile radius of where I lived, and I made it a goal to see all of them. I'd always bring a pair of binoculars, hoping to spot a variety of wildlife. There are plenty of animals out there that are incredibly scarce in other parts of the country, such as bobcats and Corsac foxes. I also wanted to use the binoculars to spot areas ahead that could be treacherous for the dogs. I did my best to avoid danger.

I had only been in town for a couple of months before I experienced the most unsettling sight of my life. I was walking along a ridge on a brisk spring day when I noticed my dogs stopped their strides. It wasn't unusual for one of them to be captivated by the rustling of a nearby squirrel or deer, but I could immediately tell this was a different kind of situation. Both dogs stopped after something caught their attention from down below. They weren't making noise. It was as if they knew it was wise to become as quiet as possible.

"What is it?" I said as I approached them, but it was like neither of them even heard me. When I arrived at their side, I casually placed a hand on each of their heads which seemed to startle them. Whatever had grasped their attention had their *full* attention. It was like they were hypnotized. They continued to stare at the vast land below, split between valley and forest. Nothing appeared unordinary until I raised the binoculars to my eyes. It felt like I had scanned every square inch of the land and was about to lower the binoculars when, suddenly, something strange caught my attention. I got a glimpse of what looked like a man dressed in an all-black sweatsuit as he crawled down a tree face-first, then ran out of sight. He was gone in a flash. There was so much overhanging foliage everywhere, obstructing my view of the more wooded area. At first, I had no way to verify whether I had imagined the odd scene.

I briefly lowered the binoculars from my face to check on the dogs. They were still frozen in the same positions as before, as quiet as ever. It started to feel very apparent that they were acting like a predator was near. I even wondered what kind of reaction I'd get from them if I were to make a bunch of noise. Would they have somehow tried to warn me to be quiet? Whatever was happening, it felt like a strange instinctual response to something that a human would have trouble understanding, especially one so inexperienced with strange phenomena.

After taking a few moments to observe them, something down below in the forest once again caught my attention. It sounded like a very beastly noise, but it was followed by what sounded like human dialogue. The dialogue sounded very choppy, but I could tell it was legitimate language. Then, there was a strange echo that followed the words. The frequency felt so odd to my ears that I'm having trouble coming up with the right words to elaborate.

Another thing I noticed about the noise was that it immediately increased my heart rate. That's strange because any typical human dialogue would not do such a thing. It was sort of like I was beginning to get the same sense for what was happening as my dogs. Even though my dogs were with me, I suddenly felt very alone, like I was totally in the middle of nowhere. Now I should mention that, at this point, I was only about two miles from the car. I am not a very anxious person, and I had never been, but suddenly, I started sweating. Everything about where I was felt wrong. I wouldn't even go as far as to say I felt like I had walked my dogs straight into the hands of danger.

All of the emotions that I just described occurred simultaneously, all within what was probably a split second. I raised the binoculars back to my eyes and scanned the area near where I saw the strange figure in the all-black suit crawl down the tree. It took me a while, but my eyes eventually landed on not just one but two more of those all-black figures. They were moving about the ground in the strangest ways that I can't even begin to describe. The best way to elaborate is to say that it almost looked like they were engaged in some strange dance. There was something very tribal about it but also very haunting. Whatever it was, it creeped me out so bad that I knew I had to do everything I could to get out of there without any of these things sensing my presence.

I then quickly lowered the binoculars from my face, only to become even more startled by the disappearance of both of my dogs. I didn't know what to do. I began whispering their names, but there was no response; nothing at all. It was as if both of them had just up and vanished while they were at my side. It didn't make any sense. How would I not have heard them run off? Noisy pebbles and leaves littered nearly every inch of where one could step. I thought I was losing my mind.

I ended up making it back to my car without any further trouble. I posted missing dog flyers in many places, but no one ever contacted me. I haven't been in the woods since.

-Street Race to Death-

Location: Pacific Northwest

Submitted by: Richard Hunt (Author)

Once upon a time, I met these two teenagers, Kevin and Dominic, who were very passionate about illegal street racing. If you have visited the Pacific Northwest, you likely know that it is not a safe environment for racing of any kind. Frankly, it comes off to me as more of a death wish rather than a hobby. You would have to be such a numbskull to risk that sort of thing. There are twists and turns everywhere, along with the narrowest streets. I've come across some of the worst accidents, especially during winter. Drivers lose control all the time around some of those bends, only to plow over a deer once they feel like they've recovered. I was very hard on these two guys the first time I caught them. It wasn't all that far from my house, and I was off duty when I encountered them. Because of that, I pretended I could have arrested them but let them off the hook with just a verbal warning. I was never that type of officer looking to be an outright asshole, although I admit that sometimes you don't have a choice, especially if you're dealing with someone unhinged and violent. This wasn't one of those situations; it was just a case of two young men having washed too many of *The Fast and the Furious* movies.

At first, I thought all that Kevin and Dominic needed was to be informed that they were risking getting in serious trouble, as well as harming themselves and others. I had no clue that they would fall victim to an even more violent circumstance than I could've imagined. I wish I could've done more to help, but I feel all right about the situation for trying to reason with them on more than one occasion.

Anyway, I received a call late one night from one of my colleagues, explaining that he came across the wreckage. I could tell by the sound of his voice that this accident was significant. Like myself, he was used to seeing some brutal outcomes of vehicle collisions. But I just knew this one was different. Furthermore, I had a feeling that it involved Kevin and Dominic because the location of the accident was close to where I had encountered them both of the previous two times.

I could not believe my eyes when I pulled up to the scene. Right away, I saw the massive boulder protruding halfway out of the windshield. There was blood and shattered glass everywhere. Something else had caused the other car to lose control and barrel roll into a gully about fifty yards up the street. It didn't take a rocket scientist to develop a theory for what happened. I didn't need to see any further evidence to know that a sasquatch was involved, possibly more than one of them.

It wouldn't be at all surprising if the creatures got irritated enough to put a stop to the street racing. Perhaps there was a mother with her offspring nearby, and she just couldn't bear the noise anymore. People should understand how quickly this species will act if they're irritated. If you are ever in the woods and you piss one of these things off, you better pray that it decides to go the other direction. Because, if not, you're as good as dead.

"What do you think happened here?" my colleague, Officer Rice, asked. I could tell he was all shaken up. That's where things got complicated. Although I was pretty confident about what had happened, I was reluctant to say a single word about that truth. I had already learned about the existence of these creatures during a horrific incident at an older woman's house (I talked about that encounter in my last book), and I also learned that our department was under strict guidelines regarding disclosure about that kind of stuff.

In a nutshell, we were not allowed to be open about that stuff. Because of that, I felt awkward discussing what was right in front of us. For all I knew, Officer Rice didn't know a single thing about sasquatch. The only people we were allowed to speak to about that topic were our superiors, and even then, we could only do it if they were the ones to initiate conversation. Eventually, I learned that that rule wasn't taken quite as seriously as I had initially imagined. It turned out to be more so that department members keep said discussions on the down-low. However, the situation involving the street racing teens happened shortly after my first bigfoot encounter, so I was still learning the ropes on how to handle all of this. It just didn't seem wise to draw attention to yourself by blabbing about that kind of thing. There was nothing to gain.

"The department is going to have a hell of a time explaining this one to their families," Officer Rice remarked, his eyes still glued to the boulder.

"Just imagine the amount of strength it would take to lift something like that," I added. Another police vehicle pulled up and placed cones on the road to block traffic.

Officer Rice and I greeted Officer Boyd and showed him the wreckage. A look in his eyes implied he had a feeling for what happened. He knew damn well that there was only one kind of thing that could've used that boulder as a weapon, and it wasn't human.

Suppose the bigfoot had been residing in that area. In that case, I imagine it would have chosen it because the street was relatively secluded, close to water, and there were plenty of nearby rock formations to provide shelter during storms. Because of how isolated the road was, other wildlife frequented the area at ease due to the limited traffic.

Therefore, it wouldn't be unrealistic for a sasquatch to expect roadkill from time to time. There had already been a few accidents on that street since I started working for that department. The previous ones involved deer or even moose getting struck by cars. Those are, without a doubt, some of the nastiest scenes you can come across as an officer of the law; however, nothing compared to this one. This accident involving the two street racing teenagers was hands down the goriest traffic-related incident I've seen to this day.

After additional personnel arrived, I was preparing to end my shift when Officer Rice commented that he thought he saw movement in the woods alongside the road. I turned my head just in time to glimpse something dark move out of sight. Whatever it was, it seemed to be intent on remaining hidden. If it hadn't been for the situation at hand, I probably would have assumed it was just a black bear, judging from the color of the fur. It wasn't all that uncommon for bears to get a little nosy in that area, sometimes even demanding food from unsuspecting hikers.

I was a bit worried about what could be near but did my best to remain composed and stand my ground. But it was only moments later that someone fired their gun behind me. Agitated from having lost hearing in one ear, I turned around to check out who shot their weapon, and that's when I saw *it*. Fleeing into the woods was a giant being, covered in black hair, at least two feet taller than me and maybe three times as wide.

For obvious reasons, I wanted to draw my weapon, but my muscles seemed to freeze up due to flashbacks of my previous run-in with these creatures—the one that ended with the death of my female colleague. Although I could only see its backside, this one appeared different than the one I got glimpses of during my last encounter. There was something slightly different about its shape and how it moved. The first time I saw one of these things, it appeared to leap into the woods, whereas this time, the creature ran much like a human, only maybe two or three times as fast.

In any case, it was a jaw-dropping site even though I already knew of their existence. Honestly, I don't think that's something that ever gets old. I do not believe that you can ever get used to that revelation; there's just something about how we've been brought up in this society that trains our minds to clash with such notions. That is why everyone who encounters a bigfoot seems to never fully accept it, regardless of what they may tell you. And I can 100% relate to that.

I was so lucky that that other officer was keeping watch; otherwise, it's hard to think about what might have happened. I had my back turned, and that thing was right behind me. It so quickly could have been lights out for me before I had any clue what was happening. It's simply amazing how sly they are; it was utterly undetectable as it crept up upon us. The only reason anyone noticed it in that particular situation was that the officer happened to turn around in time.

Later, I found out from him that he didn't have any idea it was there until he casually turned his head. I also think the other one caused the commotion on the other side of the street to focus our attention in that direction. Therefore, it would be even easier for the attacker to sneak up behind us.

Officer Rice radioed in for backup, explaining that an enormous two-legged animal had just tried to ambush us. Judging by the way he spoke about it, I right away knew that he didn't have any previous experience, at least that he knew could be tied to bigfoot. Even though we soon had a brigade of armored officers, waiting for them felt excruciatingly long, especially when considering how quickly these creatures can take you away if they please.

I'm sure all of us wanted to leave as we huddled together on the street, but it was department protocol for us not to leave behind a fresh crime scene, even if the perpetrator was still there, which, in this case, it likely was. It was standard that you call in for help and then follow additional guidelines to protect yourself before backup arrives. I find it interesting that none of us wanted to get inside our vehicles. Since we had to stick around, it was like we knew we could so quickly get squashed inside those squad cars. In a way, it would have made us sitting ducks, the equivalent of allowing the bigfoot to shoot fish in a barrel.

I remember feeling so curious about where the armored professionals came from. It was as if they showed up out of nowhere, ready for chaos. Situations involving Bigfoot have been the only ones where I've even glimpsed this type of personnel. Even their armored vehicles were mysterious. I had never even seen anything quite like them driving along the streets where I worked. It just wasn't the type of place that you would ever expect to see anything like them. Those vehicles looked more like something you would find in a war zone. Quite honestly, I don't even know what to call them, but there were two of them.

Amazed, I watched as the man exited the back of the vehicles in a very soldier-like fashion. They then proceeded to form a perimeter around the crime scene. For every three men, one of them had their attention turned inward, each one armed with an assault rifle. They were prepared to take down something large and powerful.

It was hard to tell if these men were used to this type of incident or just really well trained, obedient, and calm, no matter the situation. It was impressive. I stood there, wondering how anyone even gets on the path toward becoming part of these special operations units. If a small town like mine had personnel like this ready to go at any given moment, that made it seem like every town must be equipped with the same thing.

Of course, most urban areas have swat teams ready, but something about these men was different. They were definitely the kind of personnel reserved for extra special occasions, the ones that seldom occurred. While I marveled at their presence, I soon found out why they packed so many of those men into these armored vehicles.

A disturbed and unsuspecting man's scream echoed from the sky as he was seemingly ripped into the treetops. It happened off to my right side, and I still didn't have time to swivel my head in that direction before the soldier was gone.

I found it interesting how not even a single shot got fired after that happened. That's how quickly the snatching occurred; it was as if the other soldiers automatically knew that it was a lost cause to spray bullets in that direction. I couldn't believe how quickly the victim's yelp trailed off; it was like he was hauled off to a faraway land within seconds, all via the use of the treetops. I found myself questioning how it was even possible for creatures that large to travel throughout the branches. How was it that the wood wouldn't snap? That notion led me to suspect that these creatures know how to distribute their weight like stealth assassins, quite possibly making them the most agile killing machines on the planet.

For a few long moments, all seemed to go silent. It was as if all the special operations soldiers knew you had to be dead quiet to have even the slightest chance of detecting one of these creatures approaching. To them, there was simply no way around that; it was the only possible strategy.

Suddenly, a clan of black sasquatch leaped out of the darkness, hopped once or twice on the asphalt in the middle of the perimeter of soldiers, then sprung into the woods on the other side of the street. It happened so fast that I'm not even positive I could detect how many of them were. But if I had to guess, I would say there were about five. Once again, these professionals showed off how well-trained they were by not firing a single bullet. These creatures moved so swiftly, but I don't think there would have been a chance that even the world's best marksman could have landed a shot at that moment. Additionally, it seemed apparent that these men knew the creatures were fleeing. They seemed to agree that even if they were to shoot and kill one of the creatures, all that would do is invite more human casualties.

That marked the first time it became evident to me that even our best soldiers aren't used for hunting these things but are instead there to form a shield. If the intention were to hunt and kill bigfoot, I would have seen bullets flying in every direction that night. But it more so seemed that the men were summoned to ward the creatures off, to help minimize the number of lives taken. That was when I recognized the respect that government has for these creatures. It's almost like the officials who know of them are well aware that they are physically superior in every way, leaving us with only the mere hope of being able to defend ourselves when encountering one of them. Perhaps that notion explains why these animals aren't on official public record. They don't want word to get out that, for the most part, we are no match for these things. Of course, all of this was speculation at the time, and I did come to learn quite a few other aspects in the future, but it still does seem clear to me that what I just talked about is part of the truth. But no, if you're wondering whether that rule has ever been presented to me by a government official, it hasn't happened.

Because I had recently had two dangerous encounters with these creatures, I started to question whether their overall population might be growing. Or, maybe they had started to feel a little more confident in that area and not care so much about limiting their interaction with humans. If either case were true, that would be very hazardous for anyone who lived around there. And I felt like there was so very little I could do to protect our citizens. I was so underprepared for anything like this.

Eventually, everyone at the crime scene started to feel a little more relaxed due to the lack of sasquatch activity. Unarmed investigators were then brought in to take photos and gather evidence of the wreckage. I was told to head back to the department after that part of the process got underway.

Even though the drive back to the station should have been under ten minutes from the accident, I drove so much slower than usual. All I could think about was how a boulder had recently landed atop the windshield of a speeding, annoying-sounding car. The last thing I wanted to do was risk provoking that same outcome. I know the chances of that were very slim, but these things have a way of traumatizing you. Trust me, you think you can handle anything like it, but then you find yourself in one of these disturbing realities, and things instantly feel rawer. Just the revelation that those creatures are out there made me feel so much more vulnerable than I ever had in all my years prior. It made it very clear that we weren't meant to be at the top of the food chain.

When I finally arrived back at the station, I was in the middle of changing back into my civilian clothes when my supervisor handed me a clipboard. I was so worried that I would have to do the mounds of paperwork that I had to do the first time I learned that sasquatch are out there, but I suppose they already had the meat of my contracts. This new form was just a few pages asking me to agree that I wouldn't inform the public or any media outlets about what occurred on that particular night. I was so tired and just wanted to go home that I didn't even bother to say a word to my supervisor; I signed the forms, grabbed my backpack, and headed for my car.

While driving home that night, I realized how much more aware of the surrounding woods I had become. After you learn that bigfoot are very real, it's sort of like our forests become so much more alive. I don't think you could ever look at our national forests in the same way after coming face to face with these creatures. I decided to call out of work for the next few days. I found it hard to imagine doing anything other than allowing some of these things to sink in. I wasn't feeling much like myself; I felt more like a small child who had just woken up from the most devastating nightmare.

Since I had already experienced something so awful during the previous sasquatch encounter, I found myself wondering how many more of them would happen in my future. Part of me felt tempted to quit law enforcement and start a new career so that I didn't have to be exposed to any more brutal deaths, but another part of me decided it would be immoral not to do what I could to help people stay safe in these woods. I found myself developing schemes to let people know of these creatures, and I came up with a few good ones, but I'll get more into that in future writings.

-The Retreat from Hell-

Location: Shasta, California

Submitted by: Debbie K.

When I was going through a midlife crisis just a few years ago, I decided to embark on a journey in Northern California. I was much too used to the hustle and bustle of living in Los Angeles, and I needed a drastic change of scenery to help get my mind right. That was when I came across a few intriguing things happening up in Shasta. I had heard of Shasta many times; I knew people who graduated from the University of California in Berkeley, and they would rave about the summers they had in Shasta. They made it sound like it was the perfect place to get away if you wanted to surround yourself with nature. I want to make it very clear that I think what I experienced is a major rarity, and I don't believe you put yourself at risk by wandering through those woods. I look at it the same way I do swimming in the ocean; how many great white sharks are you likely to encounter? The chances are slim to none; let's be honest. Still, there's always a chance of facing some of the most nerve-wracking situations, so it's always good to exercise caution.

My parents raised me Catholic, but to shake things up in my life, I decided to participate in a Zen Buddhism retreat. I wanted to learn about something that I knew nothing about. I needed to learn a perspective that would help shed new light on a life that had become somewhat stale. I had been working myself to death for many years, and I desperately needed to figure out a way to implement a sense of calm in my day-to-day being. There were a handful of circumstances in my life at that time that I urgently needed to figure out how to cope better. It had gotten to the point where it felt like waking up in the morning was so forced, and that was something that I never really fell victim to, even during my teenage years. Something was off, and I'm happy I decided to go on that adventure, for it ended up making me appreciate life in ways I could never have imagined. There's nothing quite like the feeling of thinking you're going to die.

The retreat lasted a little over three weeks, and it wasn't until the beginning of that third week that I started feeling uneasy again. It was very strange; I had fallen into a new routine that I began to enjoy. I met some great people with whom I had even greater conversations, and I started to feel like the stress was dwindling. But it was like out of nowhere that something wasn't right. And things felt even stranger when I observed that others seemed to be regressing as well. Beforehand, the venue was so vibrant with optimism and positivity; now, there was a sense of doom and gloom. Even the leaders of the retreat seemed concerned. And it creeped me out when I noticed how they repeatedly glanced at the surrounding woods. What were they looking for? There was even a time when I asked but didn't receive a straight answer. It was almost as if they didn't think it was a good idea to discuss such matters. That trend carried on for a few days until, one night, I was awoken by the most peculiar noise.

It didn't make any sense; it sounded like a horse was galloping back and forth outside my dormitory, huffing as though out of breath. Every time it neared my window, I could feel a vibration in the ground, So I knew this thing had to weigh quite a bit. I lay there on my back, totally still, listening to the strange sounds for maybe ten or fifteen minutes before I heard the people in the room next to me discussing the matter. I was lucky and got a room to myself, but others had to bunk together due to a shortage of space. Initially, I was happy to get a room all to myself, but the puzzling incident made me yearn for someone to share the trepidation. What's especially interesting is that I've never felt so alone as I did at those moments. That sensation was *that* impactful even though people were only feet away from me on the other side of the wall. These rooms were tiny, not much bigger than a walk-in closet, yet I felt alone in the wilderness. I'm not sure how else to describe it.

I was so curious to know what was going on outside, but at the same time, the last thing I wanted to do was peek past those blinds and risk showing whatever was out there that there was merely a thin layer of glass separating us. If it was some kind of large bear, I didn't want to attempt it to break into my room. I wondered if maybe this thing was starving, and that's why I was running around out there; perhaps it was in desperate need of food.

Soon, I heard footsteps in the hallway. They were soft and slow, indicating that someone was trying to sneak over to a larger window to understand what was happening outside. I thought that's what it must be; I didn't think anyone was crazy enough to exit the dormitory to speak to one of the leaders about it. The retreat leaders slept in separate living quarters, and I believe the closest one was no less than fifty yards away.

It wasn't long before I heard another set of footsteps in the hallway. I felt tempted to sneak out of my room to see who was out there, but it was like I was paralyzed from fear; those

47

muscles weren't going anywhere. But then, when I heard a powerful slap against the outer wall not too far from my window, adrenaline surged through my veins, and I rushed out of the room as fast as I could. As soon as I entered the hallway, I saw the alarming silhouette. It was so gosh darn tall, even though it was ducking its head to avoid hitting the ceiling. That sight alone was unbelievable.

Shortly after my eyes adjusted to the darkness, I noticed that the tall, furry figure was inching its way toward one of my retreat mates. How did this thing get in the dormitory undetected? It looked like a giant had infiltrated the small, one-story sleeping quarters. That was when I realized that the footsteps I had heard in the hallway were from Strange figures and not from people.

The thing heard me coming out of my room, and when it turned around, I noticed that its tongue was dangling from its mouth. I couldn't see very clearly, but I could see enough to tell that it had a crazy look in its eyes. When I heard another loud slap on the outer wall, I then speculated that whatever was running around outside had been doing it to create a decoy. That enabled this other creature to sneak inside with ease. The question was: what was it after?

Even if my muscles had allowed me to run, there was nowhere to go. It was a straight hallway with doors that led to eight to ten bedrooms. The only other couple of doors led outside, which was a place I most certainly wasn't going to go. The tall silhouette began to step toward me, and that was when another one of my bunkmates opened their bedroom door, causing the perfect distraction for me to go into my bedroom and lock myself in there. It was only a second or two after I locked the door that I heard the most horrifying noises of my life. Those sounds left no question that a middle-aged woman was getting torn open. The sounds of breaking bones and splashing guts could not be mistaken.

"Run!" another one of my bunkmates yelled desperately. That was when I heard the remaining bedroom doors fling open, followed by screams of other women after they saw what was happening. An awful roar echoed through the hallway and under my door, prompting me to cover my ears from the loud pitch.

Right after I lowered my hands from my ears, I heard what sounded like at least two women getting attacked outside. I began to wonder if that meant I was safe inside the bedroom. But then I listened to the sounds of powerful sniffing aimed at the sliver of space beneath my door frame. I couldn't think of anything else to do other than stay quiet and silently pray.

I could feel tears of fear streaming down my cheeks, my heart beating faster than I ever thought possible. In my head, it was eminent death was only seconds away, but then I heard the very last thing I expected to hear in that location: the sound of a gunshot. The creepy monster charged down the hallway and essentially threw itself through the door. For a few moments, there was nothing but silence in the dormitory,

But then I heard the most heartbreaking noise of the victim crawling through the hallway with just barely enough energy to murmur the word help. Although I could barely hear it, I immediately recognized the voice; it was Lucy, the oldest retreat attendee, probably somewhere in her 80s, possibly even early 90s. Her plea for help saddened me to no end, which helped me gain some courage to open the door and see what I could do to

help. I couldn't help but halt my stride
when I saw the bloody mess. Lucy was
missing one of her lower legs and what
appeared to be a chunk of her
abdomen. She was using one hand to
crawl her way across the carpeted
floor because her other arm appeared
to be broken and dysfunctional.

Lucy yelped after I kneeled at
her side; she seemed almost
incoherent, likely thinking that I was
the creature and had come back for
more. No matter what I said to her, I
couldn't calm her. I was reluctant to
admit it, but there was just no
denying that she was a goner.
Furthermore, it didn't seem wise to
stick by this woman who continued to
scream hysterically. Although her eyes
looked intact, it appeared she was

nearly blind. Perhaps her eyesight was that bad when she wasn't wearing her glasses. It would have been perilous for me to try to help a lost cause. I looked to my left and saw that one of the entrances to the dormitory was ajar. I knew I had to find a better hiding place.

The last thing I wanted to do was go anywhere near that flailing door; however, I knew it probably wasn't logical to leave it open while Lucy refused to stop whimpering. It seemed like the perfect recipe to invite one of those creatures inside. I had no idea if there was, but I was hoping there was a basement or hidden storage closet of some kind. I wanted to find a place with some potent chemical scents to shield my body odor from predators. Maybe that was a crazy plan, but I couldn't think of anything else.

Believe it or not, I squeezed beneath the sink in the women's bathroom. I've always been rather petite, and this was a time when that paid off. I had never been good at fending off bullies in my past because of my small size, but at this point, it felt like I hit the jackpot with my genetics. It was a tight squeeze, but I sat there for quite an extended period, curled up into a ball, and listening for signs of what was happening outside. Of course, the last thing I wanted to hear was either strange footsteps or strange sniffing noises entering the bathroom, but unfortunately, that was what I got about fifteen minutes after I found my hiding spot.

Then things got even weirder. It sounded to me as though the sniffing noise crawled across the floor as if the culprit was a large snake.

"Anyone in here?" a man's voice suddenly called out, which seemed to prompt the creature just outside the cabinet doors to pause its stride. I wished to let the individual know I was trapped there, but I wasn't about to announce my whereabouts to whatever sniffed the floor. It sounded like the man's voice was coming from the main entrance of the dormitory, and there was only a slight pause before I heard the creature charging out of the bathroom and in the direction of the voice.

I covered my ears as soon as I heard the carnage. I couldn't bear to listen to another person get torn apart. While I continued to sit there covering my ears, I kept my eyes on the inside of the cabinet doors, hoping they weren't about to get ripped from the hinges. The idea of coming face to face with one of those *things* after it found my hiding spot was beyond terrifying. By that point, my lower back had begun to hurt. It started to feel like I couldn't take much more time stuffed in that small cabinet, regardless of how tiny I was.

Soon, my fear of the cabinet doors springing open came to life; however, it wasn't one of the strange creatures; it was a man wearing a bulletproof vest and a helmet. He helped me out of there, and a couple of additional men dressed in the same fatigue greeted me. The man closest to the bathroom entrance leaned his head out into the hall and announced that they had found a survivor. I was so relieved. I was also relieved to see that none of the men in the bathroom appeared to be injured. That made me suspect that the perpetrators had been taken down, and the property was now safe.

But it was while they were escorting me to an EMT that I must have spotted at least four or five human bodies on the grounds. And that was immediately after stepping foot outside; that property had to be at least ten acres; therefore, there could have been any number of dead bodies, and I wouldn't have been able to tell. But believe me, a handful was enough to make me cry uncontrollably. I could not wrap my head around the fact that I just escaped murder by something that looked so human but at the same time didn't.

The men who found me in the bathroom rushed me over to the rear of an ambulance. There was another ambulance parked beside it, and I quickly recognized the man receiving treatment; his name was Archie, and he was about twenty years younger than me. He explained he was there because he had recently lost his eldest child and needed to see life in a new light to cope with the tragedy. Not long after I spotted him, I realized he was missing most of his left hand. I didn't even want to picture what had happened to him, let alone ask him. He seemed to be all hopped up on something because, frankly, it was the most relaxed I had seen him since we met early in the retreat.

Almost every day, it seemed there was a cloud around his head; now, he looks somewhat cheerful, making me suspect he was just happy to be alive. Our little chat was interrupted by the sound of horrible screams coming from the mountains surrounding the property. They didn't sound human, but they also didn't seem animalistic. That was how I knew it had to be these creatures, the ones who broke into the dormitory and were already responsible for the death of multiple individuals.

Right after those screams emanated, the professionals who rescued us started speaking in code, and I could tell that they were now even more determined to get everyone the hell out of there. I have no way of knowing, but I've always had a feeling that many more of those creatures were on their way to the retreat property. What could have possibly triggered that attack? The retreat leaders didn't seem to have a worry in the world; the last thing I can imagine is that they had been attacked by these things before. But on the other hand, it did appear that one retreat leader watched the woods, knowing something was off.

It seemed like everyone who was found alive was immediately

driven to the nearest hospital and scanned for injuries. It certainly wasn't the busiest facility, and the staff was kind enough to open up one of their additional waiting rooms so that the retreat goers could have their own space. In there, I was able to look over everyone under the lights. Everyone in there only had minor injuries, as I assume they must have taken everyone in critical condition to a different unit.

"What were those things?" said a woman around my age, breaking the depressing silence.

"Sasquatch," stated a man named Troy, who I had chatted with in the kitchen at the retreat location.

"Sasquatch?" the woman asked. "isn't that another word for Bigfoot?"

"It is," replied Troy, "I overheard some of the rescue team talking about it." The conversation then ended abruptly. I continued to sit in silence, pondering the night. I glanced around, and it seemed like everyone else was doing the same. We were all trying to come to terms with not only the fact that those creatures exist but that they're capable of being so savage.

It was without a doubt the gloomiest environment I've ever experienced. I've never felt such an intense combination of curiosity and depression. Everyone in there knew they had been lied to about so much of what exists on our planet. Eventually, the hospital staff brought us a bunch of cots and blankets to get some rest.

The following day was filled with what felt like mounds of paperwork. I had never before seen such a bureaucratic nightmare. There were so many clauses stating that we could find ourselves in severe trouble if we were to try to expose any of what happened the previous night. Of course, everything was said in the most technical legal terms, leaving many unaware of how serious this was. Something rubbed me wrong about how the authorities handed us all those papers while maintaining compassionate demeanors. I found that to be condescending and, frankly, downright insulting. They essentially smiled at us as they had us sign forms communicating that we could lose

everything if we decided to make a
stink about the calamity.

As far as I know, nobody
protested the requests. I'm sure a few
people were puzzled by being forced to
agree not to talk about anything, but
they saw it as too big of a risk to
disobey the authorities.
Understandably, it also seemed as
though most people were far more
interested in complying so they could
get out of there quicker. Everyone was
downright exhausted, physically and
mentally.

For months after the incident, I
experienced such a wide range of
emotions. I felt different than I did
before the retreat. The thought that I
would die at the hands of hairy
demons did something to reset my

mind. Suddenly, I was so thankful for the people I encountered daily. Even the people who irritated me seemed to have a renewed aura in my eyes. A part of me believes that fate put those creatures in my life to grant me a new sense of appreciation. Life works in mysterious ways. Of course, I feel terrible for the victims and their families; I would never wish such a vicious death upon anyone, even my worst enemies.

I will forever wonder what it was that pissed off the sasquatch enough to attack a spiritual monastery. Could it be that they were desperate for nourishment? I'm sure some people wonder why they didn't just break into the kitchen and steal all the food. Perhaps they did that as well; however, the kitchen only contained vegetarian items, as the monastery inhabitants never consume meat. It would only take a glimpse of these creatures to know that they are carnivores or omnivores. I very likely could have dealt with a group of misfit sasquatch deserted by their clan. Maybe they weren't knowledgeable enough to locate other meat sources? I'm just throwing some guesses out there; obviously, I have no idea what I'm talking about.

How is it not general knowledge that these creatures live among us? That is my biggest question related to the subject. How many of these kinds of things happen so close to our backyard, yet we never hear about them? The blatant coverup certainly leaves a lot to be desired. And I don't know if we will ever get to the bottom of it.

-The Hermit and the Beast-

Location: Douglas, Michigan

Submitted by: Anonymous

I lived in rural Michigan for nearly three years when I was just a boy. About a hundred yards east of our house was the craziest neighbor, or so I thought. It turned out he dealt with something that would make almost anyone lose their mind.

We didn't even know our neighbor; he seemed to be a hermit who preferred to talk to no one. The only times I ever even saw what he looked like was when he occasionally drove by while I was riding my bike or when we passed his house, and he happened to be outside gardening or tending to his animals. Strangely, his livestock consisted of llamas or alpacas; I'm not quite sure how to differentiate between the two. And they were so far away from the road, making it hard to observe their characteristics. For the most part, the craziness that occurred on that property seemed to revolve around those barnyard animals.

On a couple of occasions, we drove by the house and saw the man burying the remains of his animals. There was even one time when I thought I saw him burying a severed head and neck of one of those animals, but my mom tried to convince me that my eyes played tricks on me. I think she worried that I saw things far too gruesome for my young age.

On several occasions, my family woke to our neighbor screaming in the middle of the night. We would hear all sorts of things like doors slamming, car horns beeping, profanity, and the strangest part of all: raspy roars. Although we never wanted to check on the man ourselves, we called the police once or twice, asking them to check that he was okay. I remember how there was one night when a squad car was parked outside his house for a while. It was apparent that the officer and our neighbor were out there with flashlights, surveying the area.

My father would always comment about how it had to be either wolves or coyotes attacking our neighbor's animals; however, I don't think there were ever any wolves around that area. Additionally, the roars and growls didn't sound like something that would come from typical local predators. These sounds were different; there's just no question. Well, one night, we finally found out what had been causing so many problems for the old hermit.

My family had a bit of an obsession with playing board games. So, it wasn't uncommon for us to sit by the fire on the weekend nights and

72

play games like *Yahtzee*, *Monopoly*, *Clue*, etc.

"What was that?" my mother asked when something outside the window caught her eye.

"What, Dear?" my father said, concerned by the look in her eyes.

I remember telling them that I was scared before even seeing anything. Something about the energy in the room got to me. It never really scared me when things were happening at my neighbors in the middle of the night, and I'm guessing that's because I felt that our neighbor's property was far enough away. That new moment felt so much more alarming, and I knew something was wrong; we were in danger.

It was hard to get a good look at whatever was happening outside unless we turned off the interior lights while simultaneously switching on the exterior lights. Well, as soon as my mother turned off the interior lights, we saw the creepy monster staring at us from just beyond our backyard deck. I think we all would've screamed had it not been for the fact that we were stunned. That beast was so shocking to look at; its long snout and pointed ears atop a human-like body were challenging to comprehend.

"Go to your room," my father commanded of me. It seemed to take every ounce of strength he had to get those words out. I wanted to do as I was told, but I couldn't move. It was like being in one of those nightmares where you want to run away from something or use the appropriate motions to defend yourself, yet you can't control your muscles. Or, you have *some* control, but you move at a snail's pace, making it impossible to escape.

Whatever this thing was, it had had a werewolf-like face, a muscular torso, all-black eyes, and was probably somewhere in the realm of 6 1/2 to 7 feet tall. I'm not sure how long the monster stood there staring at us, but when it disappeared, it was within the blink of an eye. None of us saw where it went or even in which direction. There was something so ghostly about this creature, like it had supernatural abilities. It was that, or we were just so shocked by its appearance that our brains couldn't keep up with what was happening.

My father then scooped me up and carried me to my bedroom. My mother followed closely behind. After placing me on my bed, they quietly closed the door and hung out near the railing that overlooked our foyer. There were quite a few windows surrounding our front door, so they must have been keeping a careful watch for any signs that the monster was still around.

As anxious as ever, I sat there on the edge of my bed, awaiting my parents' instructions. I must have waited there for around thirty minutes before my mother reentered the room. She told me that they glanced out of as many windows as they could sneak up to and saw no signs of the beast. I'm surprised that that creature didn't try to bust into the house. It so easily could have made its way in if it wanted to. And there was a look in its eyes that warned me that was what it was about to do, but at the last second, something seemingly deterred it. What could that have been? My parents never possessed firearms, and nobody attempted to intimidate the bipedal animal as far as I can remember. The only theory I can come up with is that it had already satisfied its hunger, and I will now get to why.

I almost can't believe we dared to get in our car, but we drove by our neighbor's house the next day and noticed a few broken windows. Later that same day, we spotted a bunch of emergency vehicles parked in his driveway. Curiosity prompted us to get back in the car and drive up the street to look at the scene from another angle. We went by just as paramedics were bringing the dead body outside. They hadn't yet put him into the body bag, and we could see that he was missing an arm and his shredded clothes.

Also, I could tell that he looked to be at least a few days deceased. The body looked much whiter than usual, almost as if frozen. It was such a grim sight that I don't think I will ever be able to get out of my head. Luckily, it was from far enough away to the point where I didn't have to see any other details. I'm sure that would have been an even more revolting image. That old man never looked like he was the cleanest of people, so I can only imagine what his decaying body looked and smelled like up close.

After connecting those dots, I don't think it's crazy to theorize that the bipedal, wolf-like creature made its way into our neighbor's home and took his life. I doubt my parents ever called the Police Department to inquire about what had happened, but I don't think honest details from the investigation were disclosed to the public. My mother did end up finding the listing in the local obituary, but I think it merely said something about the guy dying of old age. That's pretty suspicious; I've never heard of anyone getting their arm ripped off shortly before dying of old age. That was when

I became rather dubious about how much factual information is given regarding mysterious fatalities.

Shortly before we moved out of town, my father claimed to be driving home from work when he spotted an animal resembling the wolf-like monster we saw outside our house. He said he saw it just before it disappeared into the woods from many yards away. He also said it appeared to be carrying a dead animal in its mouth, but the sighting was so brief that he couldn't tell what it was. I often wonder how many people in that area have seen the creature. Are there more than one of them? If so, how are they so good at escaping publicity? If you think about it, it's not that surprising that they can remain so stealth. There are thousands of mountain lions in this country, yet people rarely encounter them. Hypothetically speaking, even if there were twenty members of a rare species, think about how difficult it would be to track them down. In a way, it would be miraculous to come across one.

Looking back at it, I'm eternally thankful that we didn't stick around that area. The thought of either of my parents or both experiencing a similar fate to our old neighbor is incomprehensible. I can't imagine what I would have done had I gotten dropped off by the school bus one day to discover that a savage animal had broken into my house. Without a powerful firearm, there is no chance that any human could defend itself against what we saw that one night. That thing was created to be a killing machine. Some of you might think I'm crazy for saying this, but I don't think even a grizzly bear would stand a chance against it. I only saw the monster for what was probably just a few seconds, but I could tell by its appearance that it was stronger and more intelligent than any known well-known predator.

I also wonder if anyone ever moved into our neighbor's house. For all I know, there have been multiple occupants. It would be interesting to find out if anyone else has glimpsed the bipedal beast.

-Tree Gorillas-

Location: Mount Airy, North Carolina

Submitted by: Jennifer T.

I'll start by clarifying that I'm not positive that what we saw were sasquatch; however, I think you'll find it hard to speculate that they were anything else. I also believe the species to be primarily nocturnal, and I will tell you why.

In the summer of 2009, my boyfriend, Devyn (now my husband), and I spent most of the summer in a remote cabin. It was a smaller structure planted on nearly an acre by the famous Blue Ridge Mountains. It was a spectacular place to decompress. I've always been an outdoor enthusiast, but never have I felt closer to nature than I did during the start of our vacation in Mount Airy. Since we lived in Charlotte, we thought we needed a lengthy break to calm our minds. For a few years leading up to that point, Devyn and I had day jobs five days a week and then bartended on the weekends for extra income. Fridays were especially tiresome because I usually only had about an hour break between gigs.

We did this because it felt like we were drowning in college debt like so many other Americans. Embarking on our cabin adventure was a little intimidating, financially speaking, but our exhausting schedules felt like they were starting to cause tension between us. We were so overworked, thus making us irritable and grumpy when the relationship used to be anything but. I remember how we both felt instant relief when we arrived at the cabin; it was like we immediately saw each other in the same light as we did when we first fell in love. It was heavenly. That first week was as decompressing as possible, but it wasn't very long before something so strange and unexpected manifested.

The first time we heard the whoops was while hanging out in a rowboat on the lake beneath the stars. At first, it sounded like a single whoop was echoing across the water and traveled an impressive distance, but soon we realized that two animals were communicating back and forth across the lake. Although we had never heard anything like it, I got the impression that something was searching for a mate.

The noise was mysterious, but I wouldn't say anything about it frightened me or made me feel like we might be in danger. We were drifting maybe forty yards from the shore during those initial noises. The water was so calm that night, making the volume of the whoops even more prominent. If you've ever heard them for yourself, you know how powerful they are. It's so impressive that any organism can project sounds of that magnitude. That alone is downright astonishing. When we first heard these noises, neither of us suspected they were connected to sasquatch. I even remember Devyn mentioned how they must be coming from a couple of large birds. Even though we were all about the idea of immersing ourselves in nature, we weren't very educated on wildlife. That must've been why we weren't thinking anything highly unusual was occurring. We merely assumed a practical explanation

The moon and stars were at their brightest that night, providing an optimal view of the lakeshore from nearly every angle. We continued to scan the grounds all around us but didn't see any animals. While doing that, I couldn't help but feel like the rest of nature had, in a sense, turned off for the night. It felt like all other wildlife in the area was trying to stay clear of whatever animals were making those noises. Even the insects had called it quits for the night. When the whoops eventually stopped, we paddled back to our dock.

Not long after we got into bed, we were reading our books when we heard what sounded like a woodpecker having its way with a nearby tree, only much louder.

"Are there nocturnal woodpeckers?" I whispered as I

continued to observe the sounds through the opened window.

"Are you kidding?" said Devyn. "It sounds like something is banging a plank of wood against a tree."

His words made me realize there's no way that what we were hearing could be caused by a small bird. It's interesting how the brain tries to come up with logical conclusions, even when they're outright ridiculous. Still, we convinced ourselves it couldn't be anything *that* unusual and drifted off to sleep once the noise stopped.

The following afternoon, I was journaling on the dock when Devyn crept up behind me and put his hand on my shoulder, almost causing me to pee my shorts. After scolding him, I noticed he held a box, and he looked excited.

"I got us a pair of night-vision goggles," Devyn said. "Now we'll be able to see the animals that were making those strange sounds last night. We'll take them out with us on the boat."

So, we did as Devyn planned, but we didn't have any luck spotting anything of the ordinary that night. All we saw was what looked to be a small herd of deer lying down for the night. At the time, I didn't understand why, but I longed for a way to warn them to get out of that area, and it was the following night I learned why.

The whoops started up again just after the sun went down, so Devyn hustled to get us to the boat and row out there to where he thought we'd have the best chance of seeing something. He was the first one to put on the night vision goggles. He had already figured out how to work them because he spent the previous day studying all their functions.

"Oh my dear god," he muttered, emphasizing that he was blown away.

"What is it?" I said, but I don't think he could even hear my soft voice because of how loud the whoops had become. This time, it was clear that multiple animals were near. It was a lot of commotion, as though they were very excited by something. Before I could ask Devyn for the goggles again, a horrible screech ambushed our ears. There was no question that something had just died or was about to.

"You've got to be kidding," Devyn said, now even more stunned by the action.

"Can I please see?" I begged. My curiosity had become overwhelming by that point. Finally, he helped me secure the goggles on my head and adjusted the lenses until I felt I could see clearly. I couldn't believe what I saw. It didn't feel at all real. It felt much more like I was watching some creepy horror movie. The two enormous figures swung from tree to tree. I couldn't believe how big they were, let alone how agile. Even though I could only see them as infrared shapes (or whatever it's called), their figures resembled great apes like gorillas or orangutans.

Whatever these creatures were, they had massive barrel chests, long arms, and legs that were significantly smaller in comparison. Another one on the ground below appeared focused on some other much smaller figure that also had a heat signature. At first, it was a bit confusing to tell what the two up in the trees were tossing back and forth to one another, but I soon realized it was a small deer, quite possibly a fawn. It wasn't clear if it was all the way dead, but either way, it was about to be.

Something about everything I was watching started to feel really dark. In a way, it felt like I was seeing something I shouldn't. I would even go as far as to say something about that sighting made me feel depressed.

Everything became gloomy. I don't know if it's because I was witnessing what appeared to be the playful torture of an innocent mammal, or if it was because of how devastating of a revelation it was that sasquatch exist. Because of the shape of the figures, Devyn concluded that what we were observing were sasquatch. As I stated before, neither of us has a way of verifying that theory with absolute certainty, but I have no idea what else they could've been.

The whoops went on for most of the night, which discouraged us from continuing our stay at that cabin. The following day, we found another vacation home with neighbors in seemingly every direction. That helped us feel reassured that we wouldn't be approached by anything like what we saw through those night vision goggles. I'm not saying that I think anything would've happened to us had we continued our stay on that lake, but neither of us wanted to stick around to find out.

Thank you for taking an interest in my report. Sasquatch are a fascinating subject, and I hope to learn more about them during my lifetime.

-THE FORBIDDEN REPORT-

Location: Munising, Michigan

Submitted by: Kathy B.

WARNING: Due to the gruesome nature of this report, it didn't feel right to include it in this book. It is terribly disturbing. If you'd still like your FREE copy, please visit this link:

http://eepurl.com/hQ6Y1f

More Sightings

If you're looking for more **Bigfoot and Dogman Sightings,** don't hesitate to check out the sequel!

Author's Request

I can't tell you how much I appreciate you taking the time to read my book. If you enjoyed it, I would be very grateful if you could leave a short and sweet review on Amazon.

Social Media

If you'd like to interact with me via social media, please follow my Instagram account:

@BigfootAndDogman

Author Bio

Richard Hunt lives an unusual life. He currently works as a police officer in the Pacific Northwest and had his first bigfoot sighting while on the job. The experience disturbed him unlike anything else he had ever experienced, birthing his newfound belief that the world needs to know these creatures exist.

But there lies a challenge with this agenda: many of the good people who have worked law enforcement in bigfoot-populated areas are aware of the coverup as well as the consequences that can come with trying to expose it. For that reason, "Richard Hunt" is not the author's real name but rather an alias to help protect his career.

Richard believes there's an advantage to his new hobby of writing: it'll enable him to inform readers of the most remarkable sasquatch-related incidents—all of which government does not want you to know.

Printed in Great Britain
by Amazon

81634061R00068